POETIC ROMANCE

KENYA WILLIAMS

ILLUMINATION PRESS
Atlanta,Georgia

POETIC ROMANCE

Copyright (c) 2021 by Kenya Williams

TABLE OF CONTENTS

The One

You the one I can talk to
You the one I confess to
You the one I spend time with
You the one who understands me
You the one who's all I need

You the one who'll ride with me
You the one who's by my side
You the one I cry with
You the one when I can't understand
You the one who I'll give anything

You the one I want to touch
You the one I give everything to
You the one who I grind with
You the one who I'll dance with
You the one who I chill with

You the one who I drink with
You the one who I write for
You the one who's with me
Through the thick and thin
You the one with me to the end

You're a friend that's part of the master plan
God put you right here with me
In my arms all night long

You the one who put a smile on my face
You the one I take to different places
You the one who I sing to

You the one who I hold at night
You the one who I'll fight for
You the one who I'll die for
You the one

2

Shiny Star

Stop feeling blue for what he has done to you.
Beautiful shiny star,
Bright heart;
So, don't feel used and mistreated.
Have some faith, it's his loss and somebody else's gain.

Shiny Star,
I'm talking to you, trying to get through to you.
In this life you have much growing to do.
No one knows your situation better than you.
To be happy means to love thy self, never down yourself.
You're the star that shines through the saddest time.

Love You

I've caused you so much pain,
Made you cry many times.
Over and over
Playing foolish games.
Now I feel like the fool.
I've lost the only friend in this world.
Someone I can depend on,
You are my half.
And I hope you understand
I'm here to stay.
Baby, I apologize for all I've said and done.
So, forgive me for all my wrongs.
Please give me a second chance—
See time will heal all things.
Hear me when I say,
You're the only one for me.
May I have your hand so
We can dance the night away
Let me make it right and turn
This house into a happy home.
A love I can call my own.
I love you.

With You

The first day of class
I knew she was one of a kind.
She giggles as I turn around.
She drops her head and looks away.
I heard her say, "He is cute.
Girl would you look at them eyes."
I fake it like I didn't hear her.
Class is over and the bell rings.
Walking and then I ask her for her name.
She was shy at first.
I ask. "Why are you shy and stuff?"
She said, "Here's my number.
So, call me later," and then she walks away.
Hold on baby what's your name?
She kept walking and smiling.
I'm here for you.
I want to be with you.
Can I comfort you?
Hi, this is Kenya; excuse
Me if I call too fast.
I didn't want the opportunity to pass.
I see you every time.
You had eyes on me, and I had eyes on you.

I'm so into you I don't know what to do.
I guess this is what a crush is like.
Thinking of you is like
Each poem that I write,
Only you can make it right.
Before I hang up tonight
What is your name and don't be shy.
She said her name is Love.
Heaven has sent you from up and above.

For You

I know it sounds like things between us are gone.
I guess it's a time when old things become new things.
My love won't change nor my feelings for you.
Everything I own is for you—
No one else but you.
I love and cherish only you.
My heart belongs to you and no one can take that away.
I love you and it's 2:04 am.
And I'm closing my thoughts by saying—
This is for you.

10

A Kiss

She was so beautiful
I mean everything to me
I even dream of her
At night I pray for her
Can't wait until tomorrow
When the girl next door
Will come out to play
She brightens my day
To see her and say hello
Someone to share my soda with
She took a sip and said silly you
Then she blew me a kiss
A kiss, a kiss, a kiss, a kiss…
Now I'm feeling like a man
No one can tell me anything
I'm on top of the world
All smiles and floating on cloud nine
As time passed us by
I hear her mom and she said
It's time to come inside
She blew me a kiss and said
I will see you on tomorrow.
Then I said okay.

All the Time

I think of you all the time.

Every day you're on my mind,
How can I make you mine?
I want to wine and dine you;
I'm blind without you.
Life is not the same without you.
Let's grow together,
Share moments together forever.
Never leave me.
Love and cherish me for all time.
Be mine
Shower me with love.
Loving that smile and
Missing you all the time.
Where do we go from here?
I've spoken so clear.
Can't you see I want you here?
I think of you not just an hour,
But every minute my heart beats.
All the time I say to myself,
Man! She's like spring time!
My favorite time of the season

❧ 13 ❧

Only God knows how I'm feeling.
How she sets this soul on fire.
If you can read thoughts…
How I mourn for your love,
That burns for your touch.
I'm drowning insane,
Visions of you in the brain.
So hard to escape this thing,
I wait in vain just to see you again.
All the time you are on my mind.
Damn...

A mother to a son

A mother to a son will never be alone.
A mother to a son can stand tall.
A mother to a son would not fall.
When things get rough, the love from
a mother and son toughens,
Nothing can tear them apart,
'Cause a mother to a son will never depart.
A mother to a son's heart is made of steel.
Even when things are bad, the love a mother to a son will heal.
Love goes to you both,
A mother to a son will always be.

Garden

Let's go into a place
Peace like the garden
Sprinkle water on seeds
Like flowers, our love grows
Blooming like roses
Beautiful as life goes on and on
Like the sun glows
We shine forever and ever
Through the winter, spring, summer and fall
In the garden
We stand tall
Rainy days, showers fall
With blessings and all
Life is nothing but a season
Many reasons to believe in

Relationships

Today, all I see are couples fighting each other
I think it is time to love one another
Relationships are built on trust
Must we trust? No, uh, uh! What you think?
Love, is it a mistake? No, no!
Why you, I ask?
Relationships, what does love have to do with it?
Couples are so silly
Today is here and tomorrow is a new day
So, don't feel sorry if you are in love with him or her. Da!!!
This is reality, not a fantasy
Have some faith for Christ's sake
Make that commitment and dedication to that someone
The person, he or she,
Love with all their heart
Don't give up on the fight
Come together and unite, so you share that pleasant night
It's time to fight with love
Relationships are not strength
Be strong in your relationship
Relationships are an everlasting love that will last forever

20

A Hug

To my women that struggle
Smile when times are hard
Positive when things are negative
Loyal all down to the end
A hug to you all
For the drama we put you through
Day to day living
And holding us down
Raising our children and more
Nursing and molding us to men
Thanks for supporting us
Love is due because the heart is true
A hug just to make it through life
The world is hard out here
Loving us unconditional
Gives men a means to life
Thanks for believing in us

What Makes A Girlfriend

What makes a girlfriend?
A girl you will hold, love, and care for life
A girlfriend
The woman who you would call your wife
A girlfriend is the one you would honor
and love with all your heart
A girlfriend's love is unconditionally there in your time of need
A girlfriend is someone who will fulfill all your needs
She will love and nurse you,
and better yet a woman that's down for you
Together share both the good and bad trials to life
The ups and downs, a girlfriend will
stand by you through the thick and thin
To me that is what makes a girlfriend so beautiful.
Cause a true girlfriend will last for centuries to come
A girlfriend

Love Unconditional

I had been through the storm…
Had it all and lost it all…
Took in the bad with the good…
Stayed even though I shouldn't…
Held on strong when, feeling like this is all wrong…
Here comes a true partner and a friend…
A love to call my own…
After all I've been through…
I understand what it means to love unconditionally…
Relationships, a working condition…
Like rain to sunshine…
You make life so much brighter…
I'm happy and life is better…
The heart feels so right…
Together we can make it right…
Side by side I choose you as my wife…
Taking a step into a new direction…
I take honor as a husband and provider…
For the rest of my life give love, protection and affection…
Our lives are complete with God's blessing…
May our marriage be forever lasting…?

A Chance

God you have given me one of the
most beautiful things in the world
I know forever my life will never be the same
This baby completes my family
I'm honored to take the role of being someone's father
I know it's not going to be easy
I'm a man of faith and with You all things are possible
I'm asking You to guide me to the righteous path
So I can become that father and husband
To my wife and child
I'm grateful to be given a chance to see life on a different level
A level in which I have never gone
I pray not only to be a father but to be a great one
I thank You from the bottom of my soul
This boy or girl
So he or she can grow strong and healthy
In Your name, the Father and Son I pray

28

A Baby

I can't wait to hold, touch, cuddle
A moment to share, a chance to show the love that was given
The word to say, a joy, blessing
Our own creation
Something she and I conceived
Life has been wonderful
Through the ups and downs we smile to each other—Like
wow!!!
A baby girl into this world
We found treasure and peace
Happy days at last
Lord, rain down Your shine and shower us with Your blessing
A baby, our way to a better life
Happy inside, joy in our heart, and the warmth in our soul
In our arms, to raise and nurse
Give her the things we didn't have
A home, a father and mother together, a family that prays
Through stormy weather - parents that care, who love
Welcome into this world
Our baby girl

Leave Him

Hey, what's wrong?
Why are you looking all down?
What has he done this time?
I'm so tired of you crying.
Why won't you just leave him?
He keeps doing this to you;
Talking to you that way.
But you choose to stay.
Crying and can't sleep—
Leave him because you don't need him.
Life can be so much better.
You deserved way better.
Someone so beautiful,
With much to offer,
I just want to chat with you.
I can treat you better
And love you like no other.
Leave him, I can make it sweeter.
With me security, compassion, understanding, maturity
Your love, my top priority,
All cards on the table…
What's it going to be?
All you need is me.

No more drama and life can be normal.
A man who cares and that'll do for you,
A chance to show a side of love,
Something like a hug,
Beautiful as a butterfly,
See I value your smile,
Leave him.
A clown, something you don't need.
So don't cry dry your eyes,
Let me wipe the tears away.
See there is another way.
Let me take you away from him.

Hold On To You

All I do is think of you
Can this be true?
A new found friend,
Love, a treasure I see in you.
Forever lies the pleasure in you,
The discovery of a woman,
Special when I look at you.
No one carries a smile like you do.
That's why I'm holding on to you.
Because I can't let you go,
Wish I can ease the pain
From the things you go through.
May I intrigue you?
For who you are,
Everything a man needs.
I have problems letting you go
Don't want to be without you.
It's hard but I try.
I don't want to give up.
I'm hoping that one day,
Through the storm,
You and I can get it together.

Happy B Day

The sun is shining.
I know when you get this message,
You are smiling.
The timing is off, but your friend is on time.
Happy B Day!
For all the times we stayed friends,
Here's something that'll put a smile on your face.
On such a beautiful day,
Again from your friend,
Happy B Day to a special lady.
You'll always be forever in my
Heart

Golden Wings

Angels with golden wings, looking down
From the tress of Heaven, soaring above the clouds.
Where the sun shines bright.
A place of love
Living outside, above the sky, doves fly.
The sweet sounds of the humming birds,
Songs of peace and love.
Angels play the harp and melodies flow.
A place to go where flowers grow and souls glow
Heaven, a home I look forward to
One day be united with mothers and fathers
Of today and yesterday
Living only to earn my golden wings.

Bring Your Body

Come here and let's take it slow
Loving that dress you wear…aww
You looking good to me
Appealing while watching you
Bring your body here
Can I touch you?
Smooth as I rub you
Like some honeydew
You taste so sweet and new
Making love like the veterans
Lance you with some ecstasy
Pleasure I'll take you there
Measure I can hardly wait
Bring your body here
As I lay you here
Whisper things you like

Exhale

I know it's your first time
I'll be gentle
Relax as I kiss you
No rush, we can take our time
May I hold you closer?
Breathe, exhale everything, it's alright
Take all the time you need
Listening to some slow jams
It's on for tonight
So kick back and unwind
As we explore the wonders
Being grown and alone
Exhale, exhale
No kissing and tell
No one has to know
It's just me and you all night
See no ring from the phone

My parents are gone
And won't be back in until later on
You seem a little nervous
Let's turn the lights down low
Lean back and let go

Both bodies touch
As we take it slow
Exhale and let it flow

Coming Through

She called me about 2 o'clock
She said to come by her spot
So I hopped into my ride
Doing 80 down the highway
I can't wait to see Ms. Lady
I'm coming through because
I know you've been waiting
I hate to keep you disappointed
I'll be there in a moment
Around the corner in a hurry
No longer feeling lonely
No worries my car is outside
In my mind as I undress you
So motivated when I step through the door
You are so sexy I can't even ignore
Looking good in that lingerie
To myself I got you all alone

All that talking has gotten me in the mood
Modeling that see through
It's so hard when I look at you
To see something so beautiful
So come here can I feel you close
Overdose as I touch you slow
There's nobody here but us
Slowly as I undress you
Lady come here and don't be shy
I want to taste that coke bottle shape
Breathtaking you got me here to stay

Dim the Lights Low

Let's listen to some music when kissing your neck
I see you girl I'm so into you
I don't know what to do…Dim the lights low
Let's get lost between the sheets
As we conceive a world of love making
As the rain drop falls
Slowly the tone of your voice moans
Sexing to a great song
I'm so gone from the way you hold me
I don't want to come back
Dim the lights low so we both can
Get ghost….

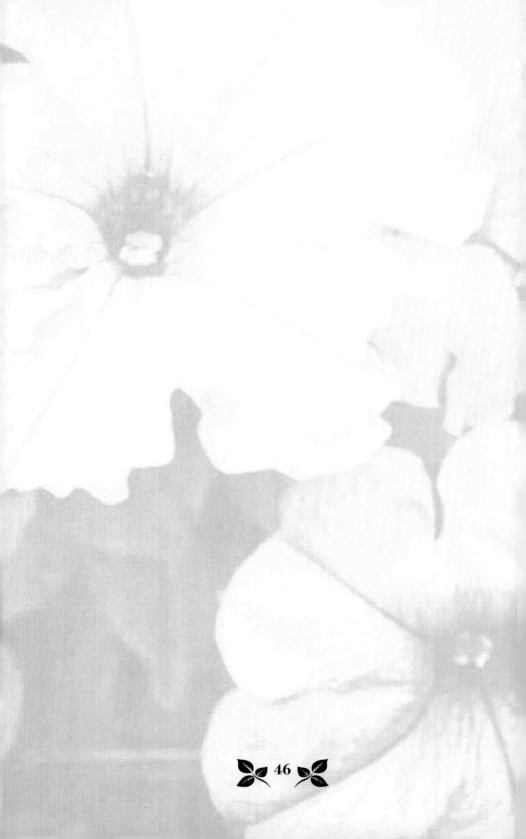

Lay You Down

I meet her at the mall
She was fine as can be
Thick thighs and all
Brown skin with the high heels on
Baby girl, what's going on?
Looking for a fellow
Because I see you're kind of lonely
Mama we can get away
Come with me I'll be your fantasy
She said a man doesn't mean thing
I want to hang with you
Because I'm down with you
We can do this thing if you want to
Take you places that you want to see
Bump your man, I'm the one who'll please you

Baby girl is looking so cute
Flossing with me when we ride in the coupe
Hair in the wind throwing peace to your friends
Rolling on twenty's drinking on Hennie
The woman that is down with me
Brown skin I'm addicted to your thighs and heels
Catching chills when I kiss you
And missing me when I'm not around
The pleasure is all mine

Love Making

All I want is to kiss you, hold you, and caress you
Love making is something we both have
Love making is when you touch me
Love making is the greatest experience you and I have had
Love making, a chance for me to show you what I am all about
Love making is something you and I share when we are together
Love making is the essence of life
Love making is the odyssey of love
All I want is to kiss you, hold you, and caress you
Love making

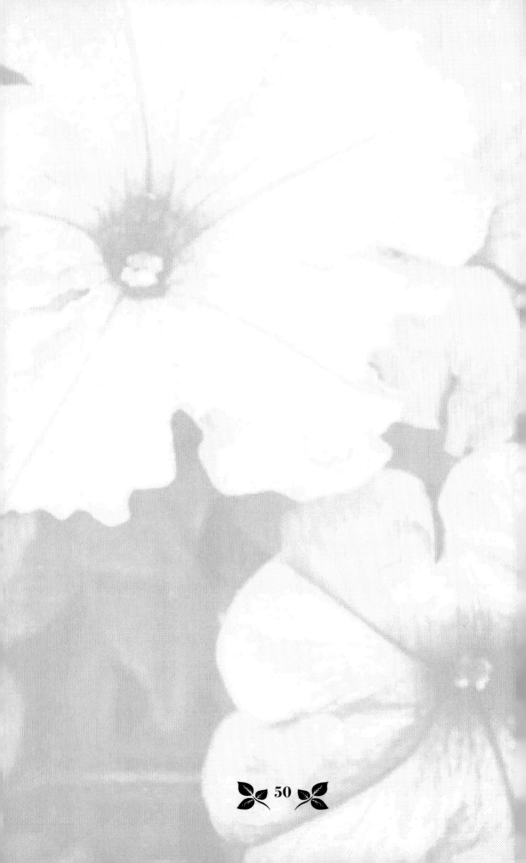

Tonight

Relax and sit next to me
Why we sip on this Hennessey
I'm feeling your vibe
When I'm rubbing them thighs
My nature rise so can I come inside
Coming on strong can I make it last
Tonight I want to make you moan
Late night turning off the phone
Touching all night long
Sexing until the early morning
Come on girl this our favorite song
Let's explore so I can see that thong
Give me a chance and I bet I'll make your night
Tell me what you want to do
Touch on me and I'll touch you
Undress me and I'll undress you
Because you know what I came to do

Kissing and touching you tonight
I want to kiss and hold you all night long
Brown skin tone rub you nice and slow
Squeezing 'cause I can't let go
Hold me close and don't rush the flow
Watch this while I do my thing
Stretch you out like some guitar strings
Misery is the master plan
Switching them gears as I improvise
I want to smash in them sheets tonight
We can crash and burn
Satisfying is the aftermath "hey"

Can We Be Friends

When I first saw you
I couldn't speak
My mind went blink
It was hard to think
Lady won't you swing my way
Sweet like ice cream on a sundae
This is my introduction
Blushing through conversation
No need to rush with hesitation
Me and you my invitation
We can go see many places
So can I put a smile on your face?
This is my lucky day
It isn't hard to tell
I see you confused as well
Expressing how I feel
Because I'm keeping it real
Lady so what is the deal
Let's meet up and have a meal

A drink or two it's up to you
Don't pass this by
The look in your eye said it all
Stop stalling what are you waiting for
The car is outside and the door is open wide
You can't deny how you feel inside
If I told you once I told you twice
Let's have us a good time

Chocolate

Dark and lovely
She is like no other
Sweet chocolate muffin
Can I taste that buttery flavor?
Stuffing
A touch of your loving
Soft and fluffy
Her body is cotton
Drip drip drip drip
Chocolate rain drops
I lust for that warm and filling spot
I'm a klutz for her coca body
Chocolate milk shake
Tasty when she walks
Fulfilling as a Coke
So let me clear my throat
Dear to me in a unique way
Ms. Lady is so delicious
And she tastes like Hershey's Kisses

I want to feel her intuition
Bite size king size it don't matter what size
Yes indeed it's good to me
Something smooth short and tall
Thick slim shock and chunky
All tasty and creamy
Sweet like a tooth ache
Special in a candy bar way
Chew you up like some Reese's Pieces
Peace to the chocolate high

For the ladies

For the ladies, the world is yours
For the ladies, your smile is like no other
For the ladies, love comes from Heaven above
For the ladies, your love flows like the river and sea
For the ladies, the flowers will bloom forever
For the ladies, words can't explain
how much you all mean to me
For the ladies, life wouldn't be the same
And the moon will shine for eternity
For the ladies, all praise goes to you all
For the ladies, I welcome you to a home of and happiness

Hey

You looking good in that birthday suit
Trying to figure out how to undress you
My thoughts going wild when I look at you
Mind blowing as I vision you
So sick can you be my Campbell soup
Thick can I have a blow of you?
Food for my soul when I think of you
No doubt I want to be with you
My heart stops when I see you
I have a crush can you tell from my blush
No rush we can take it slow
My eyes wide dulling to the floor
I'm wilding just to see you smile
I know you are tired walking miles in my mind
Can you see the sign?
Through the lens taking photos with my camera
Inner beauty makes the prefect picture
Can I place you in my portfolio?
Display you in my slide show video
Show you off like a model on a runway
I'll be your agent as you walk this way
I hope this presentation passes the test

Jamaican Queen

Dark skin short and thick
Well-built with them nice hips
On the scene walk is mean
In my dreams Jamaican Queen
So when I close my eyes
I fantasize because all I see is you
In this magazine how I lust for you
In my dream this can't be real
Reality she's a beauty queen
I've never seen someone pretty as can be
Do you know what I mean?
Sexy and modeling in a Mercedes Benz
Let's take a spin to places I've never been
Caribbean like at the beach and sands
Honestly Jamaican Queen you're the one
I rub my eyes is this a dream
I'm on my knees bagging please
Jamaican Queen you're all I need

Talk to You

Hi my name is Kenya
I'm glad to meet you
I want to get to know you
Let me stop you for awhile
Can't I talk to you?
Let me spit a little game to you
When I see you beautiful
Looking so fine
I love your style
And the way you move
Drives me wild
I had to ask
What's your name and where you going?
How you doing and can we have some fun?
And we rolling to my crib
You and I going to have a blast
Can I make it last?
You and me all night long
Hey can I talk to you
I'm digging your style and the way you move
Hold up and just listen
I've seen you before and you looking all good
I just had to say hello

Can sit back and watch a movie
You and me lodging all alone
Chilling on the couch yes!
I see you smiling
I lean over and pull you closer
And your body feels gently
I want a little some of you
I got to have you to myself
You looking good in jeans
And looking right in heels
I wonder what the panties like

The art of love

The art of love is an emotion that
I have for a girl that is so beautiful
The art of love flows like the river and sea
The art of love is a feeling she and I share when we are together
Look at the picture that's painted
See the sketching of someone so bright
Like the stars and the moon she will shine within my night
A brown coat and facial, with skin so smooth like ice cream on a
warm cozy night when the feeling is right
Let's explore the wonders of life through my eyesight
With this art of love, we can explode
in ecstasy, like a bomb of essence
With this essence, your love will bring odyssey to life.
A wife and art I can spend the rest of my life with
In this art of love, we both can lay between the leaves, grass,
trees, and daisies that bloom when the sun shines

The color of her lips is like no other
and her touch will make you quiver
No one is quite as clever as her
She is painted within my heart
and her love will never depart
She's never too far because her
love will always be here in my heart

This art lies close to my heart and I contribute
my mind, body, and soul to her
The art of love is an emotion that I have
for a girl this so beautiful
The picture of her has been painted

Unique

Girl you are so unique
You are so fine, you blow my mind
Your smile, it makes me act wild
Your eyes shine like the sunshine
I'm hoping one day that you will be mine
I offer to walk you home and with this walk we can talk
Just by being here, you have given
me the chance to express myself
I adore you, and your love I will never ignore
Hold me, cuddle me, and squeeze me tight
Just like that, now walk with me
So sweet you are
Enter the room, the door is wide open
Now come back inside
Wow!!! These roses are yours
"Happy Valentine's Day"

Spanish fly

Sexy when I see you walking by
Looking good like a slice of Spanish fly
Apple bottom round nice and tight
Aplite with that body I Like
Switching the way she move it's like
Hypnotize by the way she looks and smells
Mesmerized by the waist line
I got to have you I can't lie
Spanish fly can I be the one you like
Because when I see you in that shirt is like
So fly and I can't believe my eyes
Pretty, and all I can say is hi
Your body language got me in a trance
Uno, dos, tres, quatro, cinco
Speaking Spanish words I can't even pronounce
More ounces to the bounce
The way she walks is like iced tea that's sweet
Like can I get a bite tonight?
Spanish fly in them jeans you're looking hot
Mix spices all into my thoughts
Can I compliment you on the way you walk?

Today

Today we are going to have fun
All day you and I can roam
Today we can, explore the wonders of each other
There's no other girl who will make this heart of mine glow
Like the passion we have for each other will continue to grow
Today I can't explain how I feel
You see, I'm not ashamed to sing, swing, laugh, and hold hands
It's not a little game
We both can share a little fantasy
Today can be a special day just for you
Today we can have a whole lot of fun
Trust me alright.

On the beach

On the beach, you and me
On the beach, all alone on a warm summer night
On the beach eating a peach, rubbing each other's feet
On the beach, dreaming of someone so sweet
On the beach, you and me what a spot to be
On the beach, all alone on a warm summer night

Something Nice

Let me take you here
A place to chill
Something nice on the hills
Ice cream cones
Tinkling toes and rubbing our noses
Cuddling outdoors
Into you our soul connects
You blew me a kiss I kiss your back
Lean back as I pull you close
See the ducks walking down the shore
With not a care at all
Best friends and all
Something nice and very sweet
Sprinkling water on each other's feet
Smiling from ear to ear
Something nice because you are so sweet
Nice and sweet you are to me
Come and walk with me
Why won't you talk with me
Feel the breeze with me
Stroll the beach with me
I can't wait to see you
Jet ski with me

I'm happy feeling good inside
I'm smiling on the outside
The kids play as we pass by
I love it when you wink your eye at me
Pour another glass of tea
Something nice by the beach side
Watching the moon light
Now I see what it feels like
The view from the beach is like
When I kiss you
In the middle of the night

My Everything

I love you so very much
I'll do any and everything I can for you
You are my shiny star
My heart of joy, my soul mate,
"My everything"
Times are at their worst still we are blessed
Being together is a blessing itself
In this world all I have is you
All I need is you
My lady, my apple, my smile, my candy,
My friend, who can ask for more?
Someone I would die for
My wife someone I live for
My baby, my sweetie,
My armor joy, my hugs and kisses
"My everything"
See how much you mean to me
I love you

You Are

You are the one I love
You are the most important
thing that has happened to me
You are the girl of my dreams
The key guidance to my heart
You are the one I will live for
You are a goddess of love
For you my love bubbles like suds
I couldn't go on living without you

So Beautiful

I'll start right here
I want to feel you
I want to be near you
I got to have you here with me
In my arms where you should be
Let me hold you while you sleep
Make love to you in the sheets
All I want is you and me
All I need is you in my life
You're the one that I'll call my wife
Only one that has my back
I sacrificed everything I got
I give you my all
Together stand tall
Through the storming weather
Our love will last forever
This is special it's a blessing
My confession, dedication, devotion

My testimony

By my side never leave me
Stuck by me through the whole nine
My one only friend in this world
That's why I love you
Spend my life with you
Until the day I die
I will fight and honor you
The promise I made
When I said I do
My love is true
You are so beautiful
You blow my mind, you blow my mind

Take You Away

Let's sail away through the sea
On a ship that's far away
To be free just you and I
Around the world
Because you hold the key
Can I give you all of me?
We can cruise the night away
Have candle light and dinner
Something relaxing and beautiful
Spend some time together
Long as we have each other
No one can do it better
Who can love you better?
Forever and ever

Something Poetic

Can I make love to you?
Like I hear this music
With every breath put my flow into it
Through this pen let my thoughts go
Words pour through your mind
All over your body like wine
Oooh!!! Girl you taste
So so fine
Something poetic like wow!!!
My oh my you are the highest high
A league I can only imagine
Writing to the last ink is gone
The lyrics I speak intimacy
Your mind clear
I want to hold you in my chutches
Making love and writing non stop
May I may I, can I?
Paint this beauty
Through poetic lines

Only skin deep lies this art of mine
Heart raging rhymes intertwine
Something poetic into your mind
Expressions that drive you wild
Nice and wet
Like my ink it doesn't dry
Water down
I got that Awl
That will make you smile
Words insane with sketches of everything
From your eyes and to your toes
Something poetic that'll undress your mind

Rose Petals

Today the time has come
Waiting for this moment
I've mapped it all out in my head
Took me some time but
I manage to figure it out
How to make it all special
Here's a token of love
A rose and with this proposal
Would you be my wife?
With this ring I seal
My commitment towards you
Around your finger I wrap love
Follow me on this journey
A journey I call everlasting
Down the rose petals to life
Family, friends and smiles
The beginning of life together
A forever lasting companionship
Sailing through life together
Into the sunset we kiss to living
As the rose petals full
I'm so in love with you

Brighter Nights

No more lonely nights
Just the thought of you
Brightens my night can you imagine
Brighter Nights
When we lounge together under the moon light
Watching the midnight stars cuddling
Like lovers between covers
Could this be Heaven at its best finally I have found you
Here in my arms is where I want you to be
How nice to be held by you
Like sharing a cup of tea
Feeding each other a peach
While we rub each other's cheek
The closer you are the higher
I feel being with you
Brighter Nights

A Night in Paris

I been knowing you for a while
I want to know can I spend some time
Can I be the one that will make you smile?
Site seeing when we cruise through the town
Let's take a stroll right through the park
It's like cuddling after dark
You and me we can stare at the stars
So let me show you what this world is like
Come with me let's take this flight
I'll bring your dreams right back to life
Sipping champagne as we order something nice
Let's toss to another thing of ice
Reminiscing with the candle light dishes
Right here with me is where you ought to be
So let us spend tonight in Paris just us two
Horse and carriage as we tour the city
Beautiful as I look into your eyes
Are you ready for the big surprise?
Something special that will keep you guessing
The night is young waiting and participating
Patience there is more to come
Like art and crafts let's have some fun
Rest assured, spend the night here in Paris

Made in United States
Orlando, FL
04 August 2022

20547188R00059